The U.S. Constitution and You

Third Edition

The U.S. Constitution and You

Third Edition

by Syl Sobel, J.D.

B.E.S.
PUBLISHING

To Mom and Dad
Thanks for your love, support, encouragement, and a house full of books.

Acknowledgments

I wish to thank Judge Robert Katzmann, Judge Fern Smith, Dr. Bruce Ragsdale, and Dr. Russell Wheeler for reviewing some or all of the manuscript and for providing thoughtful comments and suggestions. Susan, Julia, and Caroline Morgan, Glen Palman and Rebecca Fanning also reviewed the manuscript, and I benefited from their advice. My wife and children are careful editors and researchers and help me write to my audience. Anna Damaskos and Angela Tartaro make my books readable and easy on the eyes.

All inquiries should be addressed to:
Peterson's Publishing, LLC
4380 S. Syracuse Street, Suite 200
Denver, CO 80237-2624
www.petersonsbooks.com

ISBN: 978-1-4380-1167-7

Library of Congress Control Number: 2018967249

Date of Manufacture: June 2019
Manufactured by: W06K06T, Tsuen Wan, Hong Kong, China

Printed in China
9 8 7 6 5 4 3 2

Contents

Introduction

If you lived in the United States in 1787, you would have been part of a great adventure. The United States was a very new country. It had declared its independence from England in 1776 and won its independence in 1783. You would have been living in a country that was just starting out.

The Liberty Bell

Proclaim Liberty throughout the land

The Declaration of Independence

Life, Liberty and the Pursuit of Happiness

Independence Hall, Philadelphia

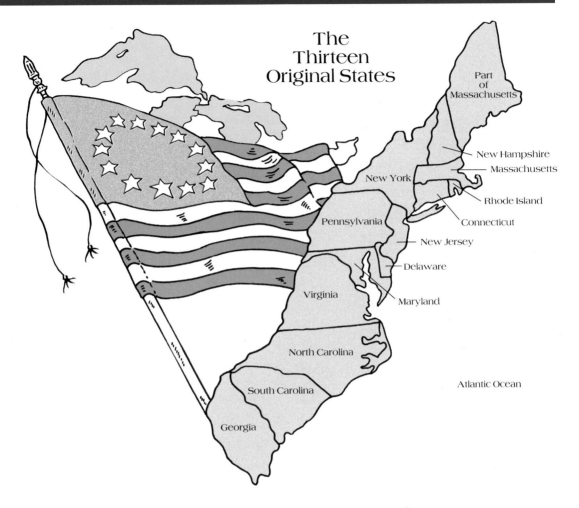

The Thirteen Original States

The leaders of the thirteen original states decided to organize their states into a league. They made rules for how their league would work. The rules were called the *Articles of Confederation.* A confederation is another word for a league.

This league, however, was not very well organized. The states called their league the United States of America, but they were not really united as one nation. Rather, each state was like its own country with its own rules. The Articles of Confederation did not have many rules to make the states work together.

So if you lived in New York, you thought of yourself as a New Yorker and not as a citizen of the United States. Same thing if you lived in Virginia, or Maryland, or Massachusetts— you put your state first and the United States second (if you even thought of the United States at all).

People from your state probably did not trust people from other states. People from other states probably did not trust people from your state. If you were a farmer or in business, some states made it difficult for you to sell your products in their states. Some states argued about which one owned certain pieces of land. The league did not have the power to settle these disagreements.

To make things more confusing, different states used different kinds of money. The Articles of Confederation did not have rules about what kind of money the states must use. Some states would not accept money from other states. So if you sold your goods in another state, you would have to accept their money, even if it was not accepted in your state. That would make it hard for you to do business in other states or even to travel to other states.

The Articles of Confederation also did not have good rules for raising money for their league. The United States could ask your state and the other states for money. However, the states could not be forced to contribute. So the United States did not have money, for example, to pay for an army or navy. If another country tried to attack your state, there was no U.S. army or navy to protect it. Your state might have to defend itself.

The United States was not getting off to a very good start. Many of the states' leaders decided they needed to organize their league better. They needed more rules to make the states work together. They needed someone in charge to make the states follow the rules. They needed an army and a navy to protect all of the states.

Leaders of the states decided to hold a meeting in Philadelphia in May 1787 to make better rules for the United States. Twelve of the thirteen states sent representatives, called *delegates*, to this meeting. Rhode Island decided not to send delegates.

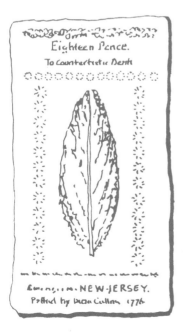

Each state had its own type of money

The delegates quickly decided they should no longer treat each state like a separate country. Most of the delegates agreed that the country needed a strong, national government—a United States government—that could make rules for all of the states. The rules they wrote to create the national government are called the *Constitution of the United States*.

The Constitution does three things. First, it creates a national government for the United States and makes rules for how that government must work. Second, it says the government cannot take away certain rights from the people of the United States. Third, it allows the state governments to keep certain rights and responsibilities. This book will explain what the Constitution does and what it means for you.

FOR DISCUSSION: Who gives the U.S. government its power?

The Rules for the Government

The delegates who wrote the Constitution were doing something that no one had ever done before. They were making rules to create a new nation from a group of independent states. The fifty-five delegates at this meeting were smart and well educated. Many of the most important people in the United States at that time were delegates, including George Washington, James Madison, Alexander Hamilton, and Benjamin Franklin. We now call these people the *Framers*, for framing the rules for our government. They are also called the Founding Fathers.

James Madison

Benjamin Franklin

Alexander Hamilton

George Washington

The Framers remembered what America was like when the king of England was in charge. They thought the king treated the people badly, and the people had no way to stop him. England was a *monarchy*. A monarchy is a country in which one person—usually a king or queen—has complete control of the government, usually for life. The Framers did not want the leaders of their government to become too powerful. They believed the people should be in charge of the government and not the other way around. A country whose government gets its power from the people is called a *republic*.

MONARCHY
Long Live the King

REPUBLIC
President

King/Queen
Born into power for life.

Government of the People
People elect leaders to office for limited terms.

ENGLAND

UNITED STATES

The Framers also believed in *democracy*, which is a system of self-government in which people make decisions by voting. But many Framers did not like the idea of complete democracy. They did not believe the people should make all of the decisions for the country. They did, however, believe in a system of government in which the people choose leaders to run the government. So the Framers created a type of government that is sometimes called a democratic republic. That means the people elect leaders to run the government.

To prevent the government's leaders from becoming more powerful than the people, the Framers created a system in which power is shared. They believed that governments have three main jobs: (1) making rules for the government and the people—these rules are called *laws*; (2) carrying out the laws, and making sure the people obey the laws; (3) settling disagreements about the laws, and punishing people who do not obey the laws. Instead of giving all three of these jobs to one person or to one group of people, the Constitution created a separate part of the government, called a *branch*, to do each job.

FOR DISCUSSION: The Framers chose to create a democratic republic to combine the 13 states under one government. What other types of government could the Framers have chosen?

Three Branches of Government

LEGISLATIVE   EXECUTIVE   JUDICIAL

The Legislative Branch

The first branch created by the Constitution is the *legislative branch*, called *Congress*, which makes the laws. People from each state elect individuals to represent them in Congress.

The Constitution divides the Congress into two groups called *houses*. One house is the *House of Representatives*, the other is the *U.S. Senate*.

The Constitution says that only Congress, and not the states, can make laws about money in the United States. Because of these laws, all of the states now use the same money. If you have a U.S. dollar, you can spend it in any state in the country.

The Constitution also gives Congress power to make laws about businesses that affect more than one state. This allows farmers and business people to sell their products in any state and for people to travel from state to state to do business. For example, if you have a favorite type of snack food in your state, there is a good chance you will find it in other states.

The Constitution gives Congress power to create an army and a navy and other branches of the military. It also says that only Congress, and not the states, can declare war on other countries.

The Constitution gives Congress power to make laws about *taxes*. Taxes are the money the government collects from the people to help it do its jobs, such as paying the soldiers and sailors and buying equipment for them. The Constitution also says only Congress, and not the states, can charge taxes on products that people sell to other countries and that people buy from other countries.

LEGISLATIVE

The Executive Branch

The second branch created by the Constitution is the *executive branch*. The leader of this branch is the *President of the United States*, who is also called the *chief executive*. The Constitution gives the president the job of carrying out the laws that Congress makes. Many people work in the executive branch to help do this job. For example, people who work in the executive branch make sure people obey the laws about business and money.

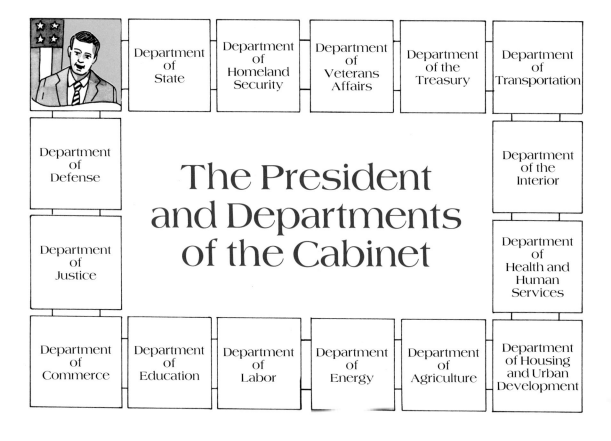

The Constitution also says the president is the *commander in chief* of the army, navy, and other military services. The president also has the power to meet with leaders of other countries and to make agreements with them.

The Constitution creates the job of vice president. The vice president takes the president's place in case anything happens to the president. The vice president is also president of the Senate. That means the vice president gets to vote in the Senate when there is a tie.

The Judicial Branch

The third branch created by the Constitution is the *judicial branch.* It contains the *Supreme Court of the United States* and other U.S. courts. (States also have their own courts.) Courts settle disagreements about the law and explain or

☆ U.S. Courts
Judges

☆ Supreme Court
Justices

interpret what the law means. Courts also decide whether people have disobeyed the law and how to punish people who have. The people in charge of making these decisions are called *judges* (and are called *justices* on the Supreme Court).

While we sometimes call the branches the first branch, the second branch, and the third branch, this does not mean they are ranked in order of importance. Each branch has equal importance under the Constitution.

The Constitution gives the U.S. government powers that the government under the Articles of Confederation did not have. The Constitution says that it and the laws of the United States are "the supreme Law of the Land." This means that the laws of the U.S. government take priority over and above the laws of the states.

Checks and Balances

By creating three separate branches to do the government's jobs, the Framers tried to keep any one branch from becoming too powerful. This system is called *separation of powers*. It gives some power to each branch of government instead of all power to only one branch of government. The Constitution also contains rules that give each branch of government some power to control the powers of the other branches. We call these rules *checks and balances*.

For example, before Congress can make a law, both houses must agree to it. More than half of the members of the House of Representatives must vote for it, and more than half of the

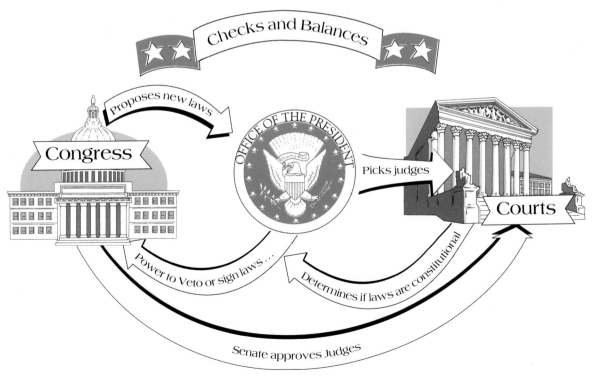

members of the Senate must vote for it. This is one check and balance on the power of Congress to make laws.

Another important check and balance is called the *veto* power. After Congress agrees to make a law, the Constitution says the president must sign it before it can become a law. If the president does not sign it, that is called a veto. If Congress still wants to make the law after the president's veto, it can. This time, however, two-thirds of the members of each house must agree to it.

What if Congress and the president agree to a law that breaks one of the rules in the Constitution? What if, for example, Congress and the president made a law that said

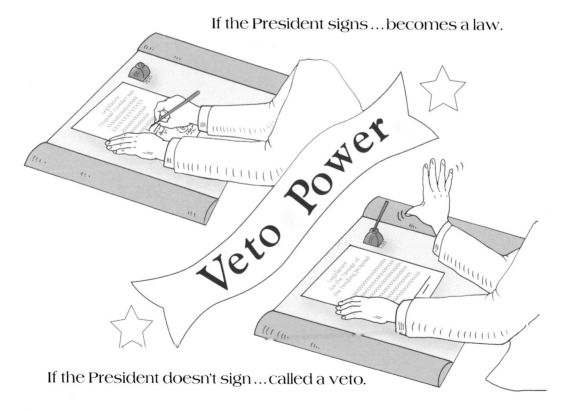

If the President signs ... becomes a law.

Veto Power

If the President doesn't sign ... called a veto.

there would be no more vice president? That is one reason why the Framers created the judicial branch. The U.S. courts decide whether laws—including state laws—are proper under the Constitution. If a law violates the Constitution, the law cannot be enforced.

That gives the courts an important check and balance on Congress and the president. What kind of checks and balances do Congress and the president have on the courts? For one thing, the president chooses people to become U.S. judges, and the Senate must agree to the people the president picks. For another, Congress decides how many courts to create in addition to the Supreme Court. Congress also decides how many judges work in each court.

FOR DISCUSSION: The Framers divided the government's powers among three branches and gave each branch power to check and balance the others. Do you think one branch is stronger than the others?

What if the president, the people who work for the president, or judges break laws or do not use their powers properly? The Constitution gives Congress the power to *impeach* high government officials. Impeach means to charge a government official with doing wrong. Impeachment can lead to the official's removal from office. Under the Constitution, the House of Representatives can decide to impeach a government official. Then, a trial is held in the Senate and the person is removed from office if two-thirds of the senators agree.

Impeachment is a very serious matter. Only nineteen government officials have been impeached since the Constitution went into effect more than 230 years ago.

The People's Powers

Some parts of the Constitution protect the people from a too-powerful government. For example, it gives the people the right to elect members of Congress and the president. In many other countries, leaders are born into power and stay in power for their entire lives.

The Constitution also limits how long government leaders can be in office. It says members of the House of Representatives keep their jobs for two years and members of the Senate keep their jobs for six years. Then they have to be elected again if they want to keep their jobs. The length

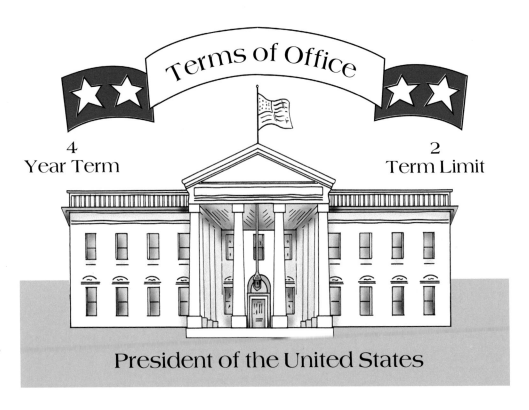

Terms of Office

4 Year Term

2 Term Limit

President of the United States

of time that a person can hold office is called a *term*. The president's term of office is four years. The Constitution now says a president can be elected to only two terms. There is no limit on the number of terms for members of Congress.

Judges of the U.S. courts, who are called *federal judges*, do not serve for terms. They may serve as judges for as long as they live. This is because judges sometimes have to make unpopular decisions. By putting judges into office for life, the Constitution allows judges to make these hard decisions without having to worry about losing their jobs. The only way judges can lose their jobs is if the House of Representatives impeaches them and the Senate votes to remove them from office.

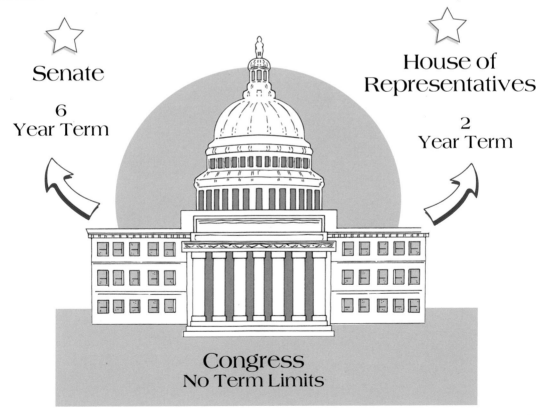

Senate

6
Year Term

House of
Representatives

2
Year Term

Congress
No Term Limits

Changing the Constitution

The Framers knew the rules they made would probably not always work for the United States. They knew that things would change. The country would grow bigger, new states would be added, events would happen that they could not predict. So the Framers included in the Constitution the rules for changing it. Changes to the Constitution are called *amendments*.

The Constitution provides two ways for the people to suggest amendments. One is for two-thirds of each house of Congress to suggest an amendment. The other is for two-thirds of the states' legislative branches to suggest an amendment. An amendment suggested by Congress or the states takes effect when three-quarters of the states agree to it.

The Constitution has been amended only twenty-seven times. Many of these amendments affect the way the

12th Amendment...1804

22nd Amendment...1951

Two-term presidential limit came after Roosevelt elected four times.

Voters vote for president and vice president together.

government works. For example, the Constitution originally said that the legislative branches in each state would elect the state's senators. This was because some of the Framers were concerned about giving too much power to the people to elect their leaders directly. By 1913, however, that concern was gone. The 17th amendment changed the Constitution so the people of each state could elect their senators.

Originally, the president was the person who came in first in the presidential election and the vice president was the person who came in second. In 1804, the 12th amendment changed the Constitution so that voters now vote for a president and a vice president together.

Originally, the Constitution had no limit on the number of terms a president could serve. However, after President Franklin D. Roosevelt was elected to four terms as president starting in 1932, the people thought there should be a limit. In 1951, the 22nd amendment changed the Constitution so that no person can be elected as president more than twice.

Originally, the Constitution said that if anything happens to the president, the vice president takes the president's place. It said that Congress should make laws to decide who would be the chief executive if anything happened to both the president and vice president. In 1967, however, the Constitution was amended to make it clearer how to replace a vice president. The 25th amendment says that if the vice president takes the president's place, then the new president picks a new vice president. This person becomes vice president if both houses of Congress agree.

- Abraham Lincoln elected 16th President of the United States.

1789

1860

1992

- George Washington elected first President of the United States.

- Amendment introduced.

- William Jefferson Clinton elected 42nd President of the United States.

- 27th Amendment adopted.

The 27th amendment took more than 200 years for the states to approve. It says that if members of Congress vote themselves a pay raise, they do not get the raise until after the next election. This way, if the people think members of Congress do not deserve more money, the people can vote them out of office. This amendment was first suggested in 1789. Not until 1992 did three-quarters of the states approve it.

These amendments help the Constitution, and the government, change as the country changes. Because so many people must agree before the Constitution can be amended, the changes sometimes happen slowly. The Framers wanted the people to be certain a change was necessary before the Constitution could be amended.

FOR DISCUSSION: Why do you think there have been so few changes to the Constitution?

The Rights of the People

The Framers included several important rights in the Constitution. For example, they gave the people the right to elect the government's leaders. They also protected the right of people accused of crimes to have a *jury* trial. A jury is a group of regular people who decides whether someone who is on trial for committing a crime is guilty of breaking the law. The Framers also provided rules to prevent the government from arresting people or putting them into jail without good reason.

After the Framers wrote the Constitution, the people in the states had to approve it. They did, but many people said the Constitution did not say enough about protecting people's rights. They believed that people are born with rights to life, liberty, and property. The people remembered that the king of England had tried to take away these rights. They thought the Constitution had to protect these rights from the new U.S. government.

So shortly after the Constitution went into effect, the people added ten amendments. These amendments are called the *Bill of Rights*. The first nine say the government cannot take away certain rights from the people. The tenth deals with the rights of the states.

The 1st amendment protects freedom of religion. It guarantees your right to practice any religion—or no religion. It says the government cannot establish an official religion.

The 1st amendment also protects your right to speak freely, even if the government does not like what you say. People can say almost whatever they want in speeches, in writing, or in pictures without being punished. The 1st amendment says people can gather together peacefully and tell the government what they want.

The Bill of Rights

- The 1st amendment protects freedom of religion and freedom of speech.
- The 2nd amendment says the states need to have groups of people ready to protect their state, so therefore it protects the people's right to own guns.
- The 3rd amendment says the government cannot force you to let soldiers stay in your home during peacetime.
- The 4th amendment says the government needs a good reason to think you broke the law before it can search you or your property or take away your belongings.
- The 5th amendment says the government must follow certain rules when it accuses someone of a crime.
- The 6th amendment says that people accused of crimes must have a fair trial.
- The 7th amendment says if people go to court to settle a disagreement, they can have a jury trial if enough money is at stake.
- The 8th amendment says people accused of crimes have a chance to get out of jail after being arrested.
- The 9th amendment protects rights that are not listed in the Constitution.
- The 10th amendment says the states have all powers that the Constitution does not either give to the U.S. government or take away from the states.

The 2nd amendment says the states need to have groups of people ready to protect their state, so therefore it protects the people's right to own guns.

The 3rd amendment says the government cannot force you to let soldiers stay in your home during peacetime. The British used to put soldiers into private homes, and the people did not like it. The Constitution says the government can put soldiers into private homes during a war but only if it follows certain rules.

The people were particularly worried about a cruel government. They wanted protection from a government that would put people into jail for no reason and then keep them in jail for a long time. They wanted protection from soldiers and police who would come into people's homes for no reason.

For this reason, the Bill of Rights has many rules that protect people who the government thinks committed a crime. These rules prevent the government from unfairly accusing people of crimes and from unfairly putting them into jail. For example, what if the police think you stole something? The 4th amendment says the government needs a good reason to think you broke the law before it can search you or your property or take away your belongings. If the police think you are hiding stolen property, they usually need written permission from a judge to search your house.

The 5th amendment says the government must follow certain rules when it accuses someone of a crime. If the government thinks you stole something, it must convince a group of people called a *grand jury* that you probably broke the law before it can put you on trial. If you go on trial and are found not guilty, then the government cannot put you on trial again. You cannot be forced to say you are guilty. The government must also follow all laws when it charges someone with breaking the law.

The 6th amendment says that people accused of crimes must have a fair trial. If the government puts you on trial, it must hold the trial quickly so you do not stay in jail for a long time. You have the right to a jury and must be told what law the government thinks you broke. The government cannot hold a trial in secret. You have the right to see and hear the people who say you broke the law. You have the right to have a lawyer help defend you. You also have the right to bring other people called witnesses into court to tell your side of the story.

6th Amendment ☆ The right to a fair trial

The Bill of Rights also protects the right to a jury trial in certain cases that are not crimes. The 7th amendment says if people go to court to settle a disagreement, they can have a jury trial if enough money is at stake.

The 8th amendment says people accused of crimes have a chance to get out of jail before a trial. They can do this by giving the government money that it will keep until the trial. This is to make sure the people show up for their trial. This amendment also says people who are guilty of breaking the law cannot be given cruel or unusual punishments.

The people who wrote these amendments knew they could not name every possible right. So the 9th amendment protects rights that are not listed in the Constitution. It says that just because the Constitution mentions some rights but not others does not mean the people do not have the rights that are not mentioned.

FOR DISCUSSION: What are some things that you do that are protected by the Bill of Rights?

Amendments After the Bill of Rights

From time to time, the people have added more amendments to the Constitution to give them more protections from government.

The 13th amendment, in 1865, made slavery illegal.

The 14th amendment, in 1868, said the states must give people the same rights as the U.S. government does under the Constitution. It also says the laws apply to all persons equally.

The 15th amendment, in 1870, gave former slaves the right to vote. It also says neither the states nor the U.S. government can stop people from voting because of their race or color.

The right to vote is so important that it has been the subject of several other amendments. Originally, the states allowed only men to vote. The 19th amendment, in 1920, gave women the right to vote. Some states would charge taxes to prevent poor people, particularly people of color, from voting. The 24th amendment, in 1964, protected the right of citizens to vote even if they cannot pay the tax. In 1971, the 26th amendment settled the question of how old people must be to vote. It says that citizens who are 18 years old and older have the right to vote.

The laws apply to all persons equally.

1870 1920

TODAY

Even today, more amendments are suggested to protect people's rights. For example, some states have approved an amendment that says women have the same constitutional rights as men. Other states believe this amendment is not necessary because they think women already have the same rights. As long as people believe they have rights that need protection, they will look to the Constitution to protect them.

The Rights of the States

The Framers wrote the Constitution to be "the supreme Law of the Land." They gave the U.S. government power over and above the powers of the state governments. They wanted one nation using the same kind of money and working together. They wanted an army and a navy to protect all of the United States. They did not want a league of separate states anymore.

At the same time, however, the Framers believed that state governments should continue to have many important jobs. Some of these jobs are similar to jobs the U.S. government does. Some of these jobs are done only by the states.

This system of two levels of government—a U.S. government and individual state governments—is called *federalism*. Sometimes, the U.S. government is called the *federal government*.

The Constitution, as originally written, gave several powers to the states. For example, it gave the states power to decide which people could vote for Congress and president. Some of these powers have since been changed by amendments. However, states still have a lot of control over elections.

The original Constitution also recognized that states would need military groups to protect themselves. These groups were called militia then and are called the National Guard now. The Constitution also recognized that states would have their own laws and courts as long as they did not disagree with the federal laws.

Just as some people wanted the Constitution to say more about individual rights, some people also wanted it to say more about states' rights. So the Bill of Rights guaranteed rights for the states. The 10th amendment says the states have all powers that the Constitution does not either give to the U.S. government or take away from the states.

State governments do many things. States run the public schools. The people in your state or community may think school should start at 9 A.M. People in other states or communities may think school should start at 8 A.M. The Constitution lets your state and community decide what time school should start. States also hire teachers, decide what subjects to teach, and set requirements to graduate.

States manage parks and other public places. States make laws about buying and selling land, houses, and office buildings. States decide who can drive a car and also make other traffic and safety laws. States have police officers to make sure the people follow the state and local laws. States even make laws to control business that takes place within their own states. However, the Constitution says the federal government makes laws about business that affects more than one state.

The state and the federal government also share some responsibilities and perform some of the same jobs. For example, states build and fix some roads, bridges, and highways; the federal government builds and fixes others. States run some parks and public areas; the federal government runs others. The federal government makes some laws about education that apply to all states, even though states make most of the laws about education in their state. And just like the federal government, state governments collect taxes and have budgets.

Where state power ends and federal power begins is a complicated question. Sometimes state governments and the federal government disagree, and the courts have to decide.

States also play an important role in amending the Constitution. Remember that two-thirds of the states can suggest changes to the Constitution. Three-fourths of the states must approve an amendment before it becomes part of the Constitution.

Federalism is another way in which government power is shared under the Constitution. It is another limit on the power of the U.S. government.

FOR DISCUSSION: The Framers chose to create a U.S. government with powers over the state governments. How might the United States be different today if the Framers had given more power to the states? For example, what if each state had its own army and could decide whether or not to fight in a war? What if the people of each state could decide whether or not to follow the laws that Congress makes?

The Constitution and You

The Constitution is a remarkable document. When it was written, it created a new nation and a new form of government. Nothing like it had ever been written before. Now, the government it created has lasted more than 230 years. Many other countries model their constitutions on ours.

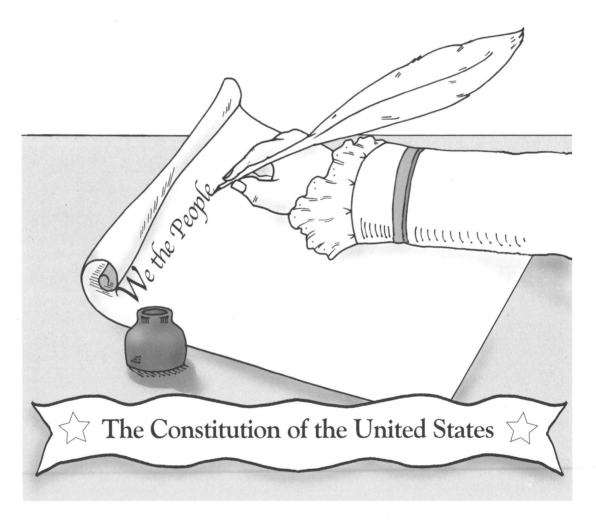

The Constitution of the United States

The Constitution creates a system of government that gives you many freedoms and protections that people in other countries do not have. Some countries have a single, all-powerful leader who makes all the laws. In our country, the Constitution makes the president share much of the decision-making power with Congress. In addition, the courts make sure the laws agree with the Constitution.

In some countries, people are born into positions of leadership. In our country, the Constitution gives the people the right to elect the nation's leaders. It also sets requirements for who can hold certain offices. Anyone who meets those requirements can try to get elected.

In some countries, kings, queens, and other rulers stay in power for life. In our country, the Constitution says that every few years, the people can choose new leaders.

In some countries, the government tells you which religion to practice and punishes people who do not practice that religion. In our country, the Constitution says that you can practice any religion—or no religion.

In some countries, the government punishes people who complain about the government. In our country, the Constitution says you may speak and write freely, even if the government does not like it.

In some countries, the government arrests people, puts them in jail, and punishes them for no reason. In our country, the Constitution says the government must follow many rules to protect the rights of people who are charged with crimes.

Protecting these rights also means you have important responsibilities. One responsibility is to vote so you can choose leaders and lawmakers who will act wisely and protect your rights. Another responsibility is to serve on juries, to protect the right to jury trials. Another responsibility is to pay taxes so that the government gets the money it needs to do its many jobs.

When the Framers finished writing the Constitution and left their meeting in Philadelphia, someone asked Benjamin Franklin, "What have you given us?"

"A republic," Franklin replied. "If you can keep it."

The Constitution creates a government of the people. Our job is to keep it going.

Glossary

Amendment: A change to the Constitution. There have been twenty-seven amendments to the Constitution.

Articles of Confederation: The rules that the thirteen original states made after they declared independence from Great Britain. A confederation is another word for a league.

Bill of Rights: The first ten amendments to the U.S. Constitution. They say the government cannot take away certain rights.

Checks and Balances: Rules that give each branch of government some power to control the powers of the other branches.

Chief Executive: Another name for the President of the United States.

Commander in Chief: Another name for the President of the United States. One of the jobs of the president is to be in charge of the military.

Congress: The group of elected representatives who make the laws of the United States. Congress serves as the legislative branch of the U.S. government. It has two groups, called the House of Representatives and the U.S. Senate.

Constitution of the United States: The rules that establish the U.S. government and tell the government what its jobs are. The Constitution also protects certain rights of the people and of the states.

Delegates: People who represent other people. Twelve of the thirteen states sent delegates to the meeting in Philadelphia in 1787 to write the Constitution of the United States.

Democracy: A government in which people make decisions by voting.

Executive Branch: The second branch of the U.S. government. The leader of this branch is the President of the United States, who is called the chief executive. The Constitution gives this branch the job of carrying out the laws that Congress makes.

Federal Government: Another name for the U.S. government. The United States has a federal government and 50 state governments.

Federalism: The system of two levels of government— a national government for the whole country and state governments for each state.

Framers: The people who created the Constitution in 1787. Many of the most important people in the United States at that time were Framers, including George Washington, James Madison, Alexander Hamilton, and Benjamin Franklin. The Framers are also called the Founding Fathers.

Grand Jury: Before the government can put someone on trial, it must first convince a group of people called a grand jury that the person probably broke the law.

House of Representatives: One of the two houses of Congress. The other is the U.S. Senate.

Houses: The two groups that make up Congress. One house is the House of Representatives, the other is the U.S. Senate. Before Congress can make a law, both houses must agree to it.

Impeach: When the House of Representatives accuses a high government official of doing wrong. Impeachment can lead to the official's removal from office.

Judges: The people in charge of the courts. They decide what the law means when people disagree about its meaning and how to punish people who have broken the law. The judges of the U.S. courts are called **federal judges**.

Judicial Branch: The third branch of the U.S. government. It contains the Supreme Court of the United States and other courts. Courts settle disagreements about the law and explain what the law means. They also decide whether people have broken the law and how to punish people who have.

Jury: A group of regular people who decides whether someone on trial broke the law. Juries also decide some disagreements that people bring to court.

Justices: The judges on the Supreme Court of the United States.

Laws: The rules that Congress makes and the president approves. Laws tell the people and the government what they can and cannot do.

Legislative Branch: The first branch of the U.S. government. It consists of Congress, which makes the laws.

Monarchy: A country in which one person—usually a king or queen—has complete control of the government, usually for life.

President: The leader of the executive branch. The president also commands the military and meets with leaders of other countries.

Republic: A country in which the government gets its power from the people.

Separation of Powers: The system of government that gives some power to each branch of government instead of all power to only one branch.

Supreme Court of the United States: The highest court in the United States. It can decide whether other courts made the right decision.

Taxes: The money the government collects from the people to help it do its jobs, such as building roads and bridges, paying members of the military, and buying equipment for them.

Term: The length of time that a person can hold office. The term of office for the president is four years. The Constitution says a president can be elected to no more than two terms.

U.S. Senate: One of the two houses of Congress. The other is the House of Representatives.

Veto: When the president does not sign a law that Congress makes. The law does not go into effect unless two-thirds of each house of Congress vote again to make it a law.

Resource Guide

Books

Many fine children's books are available about the Constitution. Here are some of them.

Catrow, David, *We the Kids: The Preamble to the Constitution of the United States* (Puffin Books, NY, 2005).

Cheney, Lynn, *We the People: The Story of Our Constitution* (Simon & Schuster Books for Young Readers, NY, 2012).

Fritz, Jean, *Shh! We're Writing the Constitution* (Puffin Books, NY, 1997).

Hossell, Karen Price, *The United States Constitution* (Heinemann Library, Chicago, IL, 2003).

Hossell, Karen Price, *The Bill of Rights* (Heinemann Library, Chicago, IL, 2003).

Krull, Kathleen, *A Kids' Guide to America's Bill of Rights: Curfews, Censorship, and the 100-Pound Giant* (Revised edition) (Harper Collins, NY, 2015).

Levy, Elizabeth, *. . . If You Were There When They Signed the Constitution* (Scholastic, NY, 2006).

Maestro, Betsy and Giulio Maestro, *A More Perfect Union: The Story of Our Constitution* (Harper Collins, NY, 2008).

Prolman, Marilyn, *The Story of the Constitution* (Childrens Press, Danbury, CT, 2002).

Spier, Peter, *We the People: The Constitution of the United States of America* (Doubleday, 2014).

Taylor-Butler, Christine, *The Constitution of the United States (True Books)* (Childrens Press, Danbury, CT, 2008)

Travis, Cathy, *Constitution Translated for Kids* (We the Books, Washington, D.C., 2016).

Websites

Here are the addresses of some informative websites about the Constitution.

Ben's Guide to U.S. Government (Government Printing Office)
http://bensguide.gpo.gov

Constitution of the United States (National Archives)
www.archives.gov/founding-docs/constitution

Constitution of the United States (U.S. Senate)
www.senate.gov/civics/constitution_item/constitution.htm

Index